United States Presidents

John Adams

Anne Welsbacher
ABDO Publishing Company

visit us at
www.abdopub.com

Published by Abdo Publishing Company 4940 Viking Drive, Edina, Minnesota 55435.
Copyright © 1999 by Abdo Consulting Group, Inc. International copyrights reserved in
all countries. No part of this book may be reproduced in any form without written
permission from the publisher.

Printed in the United States.

Cover and Interior Photo credits: Peter Arnold, Inc., SuperStock, Archive, Corbis-
Bettmann

Edited by Lori Kinstad Pupeza
Contributing editors: Alan Gergen and Elizabeth Clouter-Gergen

Library of Congress Cataloging-in-Publication Data

Welsbacher, Anne, 1955-
    John Adams / Anne Welsbacher.
    p. cm. -- (United States presidents)
    Includes index.
    Summary: A simple biography of the second president of the United States,
    from his childhood and education in Massachusetts to his marriage to Abigail
    Smith and his role in the country's early history.
    ISBN 1-56239-738-9
    1. Adams, John, 1735-1826--Juvenile literature. 2. Adams, Abigail, 1744-1818--
    Juvenile literature. 3. Presidents--United States--Biography--Juvenile literature.
    4. Presidents' spouses--United States--Biography--Juvenile literature. [1.
    Adams, John, 1735-1826. 2. Presidents.] I. Title. II. Series: United States
    presidents (Edina, Minn.)
    E322.W45   1998
    973.4'4'092--dc21
    [B]
                                                     97-39295
                                                     CIP
                                                      AC

Contents

Leader of a New Nation

*J*ohn Adams led the fight for a new country—the United States of America. He was the first person to argue that England's **colonies** should break away and be their own country. He also helped write papers that made that very thing come true.

John Adams put together the very first United States Navy. He did this to protect his new country. He also kept the United States out of other countries' wars.

As a boy, John Adams was very strong. He loved to work on the family farm in Massachusetts. But his father wanted him to learn as much as he could. So John learned to read when he was still young.

When John was 16, he went to Harvard **college** in Cambridge, Massachusetts. At first he studied to be a **minister**. Then he tried teaching. At last he chose law.

John Adams, second president of the United States

John Adams went to town meetings. He talked to others about problems in England and France. He started to think about the **colonies** breaking free from England.

John married Abigail Smith. They had five children. John worked as a lawyer and as a farmer. Abigail loved to read. She **advised** her husband about many things. When they were apart, they wrote many letters to each other.

Soon the colonies fought England for freedom. John had ideas about a new kind of government. He helped plan the **Declaration of Independence**. He said George Washington should be the first commander of the new army. Everybody agreed.

John Adams lived in Europe for almost 10 years. He worked to bring peace for his new country. Later, George Washington was voted the first president. John Adams was his vice president.

Later, John Adams was voted the second United States president. Many people argued with him about how to do his job. It was a hard job, but he did what he thought was best for the country.

After he **retired**, John wrote many letters and papers. He died exactly 50 years after the start of the United States—the country he helped to create.

John Adams was born in this frame house in Braintree, Massachusetts (now Quincy, Massachusetts). Built in 1681, the house has been kept up by the state.

John Adams (1735-1826)
Second President

BORN:	October 30, 1735
PLACE OF BIRTH:	Braintree (Quincy), Massachusetts
ANCESTRY:	English
FATHER:	John Adams (1691-1761)
MOTHER:	Susanna Boylston Adams (1699-1797)
WIFE:	Abigail Smith (1744-1818)
CHILDREN:	Five: 3 boys, 2 girls
EDUCATION:	Private schools; received B.A. (1755) and M.A. (1758) from Harvard
RELIGION:	Unitarian
OCCUPATION:	Teacher, farmer, lawyer, essayist and political writer, and diplomat
MILITARY SERVICE:	None
POLITICAL PARTY:	Federalist

OFFICES HELD:	Representative to Massachusetts General Court; Delegate to First and Second Continental Congress; Member of Provincial Congress of Massachusetts; Commissioner to France; Delegate to Massachusetts Constitutional Convention; Minister to the Netherlands and Great Britain; Envoy to the Court of St. James in London; Vice President.
AGE AT INAUGURATION:	61
TERMS SERVED:	One (1797-1801)
VICE PRESIDENT:	Thomas Jefferson
DIED:	July 4, 1826, Quincy, Massachusetts, age 90
CAUSE OF DEATH:	Natural causes

Detail Area

Massachusetts

Braintree
(Quincy)

Birthplace of John Adams

Early Years

*J*ohn Adams was born in Braintree, Massachusetts, on October 30, 1735. Massachusetts was not a state, but an English **colony**.

John was the oldest of three boys. He liked to make kites and fly them. He whittled sticks and hunted for birds' eggs. John was like his mother, Susanna, in many ways. He liked to talk and had a hot temper.

John was very strong and loved working on the family farm. He wanted to be a farmer when he grew up. But his father, John Sr., wanted all his boys to learn as much as they could. When John was six, his father taught him to read.

John's father was a **Puritan minister**. The Puritans followed a very firm religion.

John didn't like his classes or his teacher. Sometimes, he skipped school! But his father scolded him, and soon John was studying hard.

John studied for tests to go to Harvard, a **college** in Cambridge, Massachusetts. Harvard was not easy to get into. But John studied hard. When he was 15, he passed the entrance exams.

Portrait of John Adams

College at Harvard

When he was almost 16, John left home to go to Harvard. The **college** was started by a **Puritan minister**. It had very firm rules for the students.

The students were all boys. They had to get up very early in the morning. They studied most of the day. They went to bed early at night.

John loved to read. At first he studied to be a minister. But he did not like some things about the Puritan religion. So he decided to try teaching.

John graduated in 1755, when he was 19 years old. He moved to Worcester, Massachusetts, to begin teaching.

In Worcester, John and his neighbors talked about **politics**. People talked a lot about wars in England and France. Both these countries wanted land in the **colonies**.

John soon learned he didn't like to teach. He decided to be a lawyer. He studied for two years. Then, in 1758, he moved back to Braintree to start his new job as a lawyer.

John Adams studied to be a lawyer.

John and Abigail

*I*n 1761, John watched a trial about trade laws in England. For the first time, he wondered if the **colonies** should break free from England. Also that year, John's father died.

John received his father's house and farmland. In 1764, John married Abigail Smith. John and Abigail were old friends.

Abigail was very smart. In those days, most girls were not taught to read. But Abigail's father wanted the best for his children. He taught Abigail to read.

Abigail had a good sense of humor. She also loved **politics** and books. She and John enjoyed talking about the **colonies** and other countries. Sometimes, John's temper made him seem rude to people. But Abigail always smoothed things over.

John and Abigail had five children. Susannah died as a baby. The other children were Abigail, John Quincy, Charles, and Thomas.

The Adams were very happy together. John farmed his land and built up his law business. He was the farmer he always wanted to be. And he had the education his father always wanted for him.

John Adams was a farmer, lawyer, and politician.

The Making of the 2nd United States President

1735 ➤ Born Oct. 30, in Braintree (Quincy), MA

1741 ➤ Learns to read

1751 ➤ Enters Harvard College

1755 ➤ Graduates from Harvard; moves to Worchester to begin teaching

1767 ➤ Son John Quincy Adams is born

1774 ➤ Elected delegate to the Continental Congress

1776 ➤ Declaration of Independence is signed

1792 ➤ Re-elected vice president

1796 Elected 2nd president of the United States

1800 1st president to live in White House

PRESIDENTIAL   YEARS

John Adams

"Liberty cannot be preserved without a general knowledge among the people."

1758

Becomes
a lawyer,
returns to
Braintree

1764

Marries
Abigail
Smith

1777

Appointed com-
missioner to
France, serves
with Ben Franklin

1788

Elected 1st vice
president of the
U.S. under George
Washington

1818

Wife
Abigail
dies in
October

1826

John dies
July 4,
at the age
of 90

Historical Highlights
during Adams Administration

Capital moved from Philadelphia to
Washington, D.C.

Navy Department created

George Washington dies

Peace with France

Alien and Sedition Acts are formed

John Marshall is made Chief Justice
of the Supreme Court

Fighter for Freedom

*I*n the 1760s, the English **colonies** had to pay many **taxes** to England. In 1765, a new law, called the Stamp Act, demanded even more money.

John Adams was angry. He gave many speeches. He also wrote many newspaper articles about how a new government could be run.

But John believed in fairness to everybody. There was a fight called the Boston Massacre in 1770. English soldiers went on trial for shooting people.

John was afraid the soldiers would not get a fair trial. So he became their lawyer! He thought the colonists would be angry with him. But they liked him even more because he was fair. So, John was chosen to serve in the Massachusetts **House of Representatives**.

In 1773, England passed a tax on tea shipped to the colonies. To **protest** the tax, colonists climbed onto an

English ship in Boston Harbor filled with tea and threw the tea into the water. This was called the Boston Tea Party.

One year later, John Adams went to a meeting in Philadelphia for all leading **colonists**. It was called the First Continental **Congress.** They wanted to decide what to do about the English. Most, like John, wanted the colonies to form their own country. But others did not.

The Congress had more meetings. John Adams said it was time the colonists had their own army. He also said that George Washington should lead the army. War with England was almost upon them.

John Adams

A New Nation

*B*y 1776, the **Congress** agreed to break from England. They asked John and Thomas Jefferson to write a paper that said the colonies were a free country.

Thomas wrote most of the paper. He was a talented writer. When it was finished, John defended the paper before Congress. Finally, on July 4, 1776, Congress signed the **Declaration of Independence**. The United States of America was born.

Now the new country had to fight for its freedom. In the colonies, George Washington and others led the American **Revolution** against England. From 1777 to 1779, John spent time in France. He wanted the French to help America in the war.

In 1780, John wrote a paper called the state **constitution**. It stated all the laws and rules for Massachusetts. Because the paper was so good, other states used it for their constitutions.

President George Washington and Vice President John Adams's inauguration at Old City Hall in New York, April 30, 1789. George Washington is taking the oath of office.

In 1780, John and his sons, John Quincy and Charles, went to France. **Congress** wanted John to try to make peace with England. John missed Abigail and his other children. He and Abigail wrote many letters to each other.

In 1781, the United States' victory at Yorktown, Virginia, ended the American **Revolution**. But it took John two more years to get England to sign a peace treaty. In 1785, the rest of John's family joined him in France. That same year, the Adams moved to England. There, John worked to keep the peace between America and the English.

In 1788, John and his family returned home. The next year, Congress voted for the first president of the United States. This is called an election. George Washington got the most votes, so he became president. John Adams got the next most, so he became vice president of the United States!

Opposite page: John Adams spent many years in Europe negotiating peace treaties.

The President's Work

*T*imes were hard. People argued about wars in Europe and about land in the western United States. In the 1792 election, John remained vice president under Washington.

In 1796, Washington **retired** and there was another election. John Adams got the most votes. Thomas Jefferson became his vice president.

John Adams took the office of the president in March 1797. But soon he had trouble with Thomas and **Congress.**

There was a **revolution** in France. Many French people were fighting their government. Thomas wanted the U.S. to help the French people with their war. But John wanted to make peace with the French government. This decision angered Thomas and many in Congress. It would cost John the next election.

In 1800, John and Abigail moved into the White House in the new capital of Washington, D.C. John Adams was the first president to live there.

The house wasn't even finished! There was mud all around it. But Abigail had a big party anyway.

That year, John Adams picked John Marshall as the new chief justice for the Supreme Court. The Supreme Court is the highest court in the United States.

There also was another election. This time, Thomas Jefferson won the most votes. John Adams was no longer the president.

John Adams
1735-1826

Home With Friends

*J*ohn Adams was hurt and sad when he lost the election. He left Washington, D.C., without saying good-bye to Thomas Jefferson.

John and Abigail went home to Braintree, now called Quincy. John and Abigail had parties for friends and neighbors. The people in his hometown were still his good friends.

John wrote many letters and articles after he left Washington, D.C. One day, Abigail wrote to Thomas Jefferson in secret. Thomas then wrote John. At last they were friends again! They wrote many letters to each other.

In October 1818, Abigail died. John was very sad. He wrote many letters to Thomas about how much he missed her.

A few years later, John became very sick. He was dying. The last thing he said before he died was that his friend Thomas was still alive.

John didn't know it, but Thomas had died that day, too. It was July 4, 1826—the 50th birthday of the United States of America!

John Adams lost his second election to Thomas Jefferson. However, they remained very good friends.

John and Abigail Adams

•John Adams always liked to talk. Even when he was a boy, his Uncle Peter called him "the talkingest boy" he ever knew!

•There is a famous musical play called *1776* about the people who signed the **Declaration of Independence**. In one song, everybody yells at John Adams to sit down and stop talking! In another song, everybody agrees that John is "obnoxious and disliked." Even John himself knew he was a hard person to like.

•When John Adams was away at **Congress** meetings, he and Abigail wrote letters to each other almost every day. The letters were carried 400 miles (644 km) on horseback.

•Abigail Adams was the first U.S. woman ever to meet the Queen of England. But the queen kept her waiting for four hours, and was rude to her when she finally came. Later, the other women in the English court said that Abigail acted more like a queen than their own queen did!

•John and Abigail's son, John Quincy Adams, became the sixth president of the United States. Abigail was the only woman ever to be both the wife of a president and the mother of a president.

•When he was a young man, John Adams decided he would never get married. He thought it would get in the way of his career. But later he visited a pretty girl named Hannah Quincy and almost asked her to marry him. This scared him so much he ran out of the house, and never came back!

Glossary

Advise—to help a person decide things.

Cabinet—one group of people in the United States government; the cabinet is picked by the president.

College—a school you can go to after high school.

Colony—a group of people who leave their own country and settle in another land, but remain citizens of their own country.

Congress—one group of people in the United States government; the Congress helps decide laws, and members of Congress are elected by U.S. citizens.

Constitution—an important piece of paper that describes freedom and rights for Americans.

Declaration of Independence—an important paper that said the English colonies wanted to be free and start their own government.

House of Representatives—an elected lawmaking group.

Minister—a member of the clergy serving a church.

Negotiate—to talk with other leaders about peace and freedom.

Politics—the process of making laws and running a government.

Protest—to strongly object to something.

Puritan—a person who wanted a simple form of worship with strick morals.

Retire—to give up an office or job.

Revolution—a complete change in government, often by force.

Taxes—extra fees paid to the government.

Internet Sites

United States Presidents Information Page
http://we.got.net/docent/soquel/prez.htm
Links to information about United States Presidents. This site is very informative, with biographies on every president as well as speeches and debates, and other links.

The Presidents of the United States of America
http://www.whitehouse.gov/WH/glimpse/presidents/html/presidents.html
This site is from the White House. With an introduction from President Bill Clinton and biographies that include each president's inaugural address, this site is excellent. Get information on White House history, art in the White House, first ladies, first families, and much more.

POTUS—Presidents of the United States
http://www.ipl.org/ref/POTUS/
In this resource you will find background information, election results, cabinet members, presidency highlights, and some odd facts on each of the presidents. Links to biographies, historical documents, audio and video files, and other presidential sites are also included to enrich this site.

These sites are subject to change. Go to your favorite search engine and type in United States presidents for more sites.

Pass It On

History Enthusiasts: educate readers around the country by passing on information you've learned about presidents or other important people who've changed history. Share your little-known facts and interesting stories. We want to hear from you!

To get posted on the ABDO Publishing Company Web site, E-mail us at "History@abdopub.com"
Visit the ABDO Publishing Company Web site at www.abdopub.com

Index

jB
ADAMS

Welsbacher, Anne

John Adams

$19.92